NICK

Heaven touching *Earth*

Prayers for daily life

kevin mayhew

First published in 2005 by

KEVIN MAYHEW LTD
Buxhall, Stowmarket, Suffolk, IP14 3BW
E-mail: info@kevinmayhewltd.com
Web: www.kevinmayhew.com

9 8 7 6 5 4 3 2 1 0

ISBN 1 84417 484 0
Catalogue No. 1500850

Cover design by Angela Selfe
Edited and typeset by Katherine Laidler

Printed and bound in Great Britain

Contents

To my dear sister Velma,
a truly special person

Introduction

In my book *Touched by His Hand* I recalled the inspiration I gained as a young man from the prayers of Michel Quoist in his book *Prayers of Life* – prayers unlike any I'd come across before. Instead of approaching God in formal and stilted language, he seemed to be chatting with him, casually yet reverently discussing the ins and outs of everyday life. But it wasn't just the language that was different – it was also the themes of the prayers, a bewildering variety of subjects being covered: 'Prayer Before a Five Pound Note', 'The Pornographic Magazine', 'The Wire Fence', 'The Underground', 'The Swing', 'The Tractor' and many more. Such an approach came as a breath of fresh air, blowing away the cobwebs in my devotional life, for suddenly prayer wasn't limited to a few moments at the beginning or end of the day, nor an overtly religious activity conducted with eyes closed and tucked safely away from the world. Rather, it was part of being alive, each moment being touched by God's presence.

This book follows on from *Touched by His Hand* in attempting to approach prayer from that down-to-earth perspective, relating it to everyday people, places, objects and experiences, and thus breaking down the divide between the sacred and secular, divine and human. Avoiding religious jargon as far as possible, and resisting the temptation to link prayers to particular passages of Scripture – easy though this would be in most cases – it comprises another hundred prayers rooted in everyday life. The commonplace provides a backdrop to an encounter with God, things as ordinary as a stale loaf, cup of tea, exam paper, packet of cigarettes, broken window, sleepless night or knotted hankie providing inspiration for prayer. In each case the aim is the same: to ask how such seemingly ordinary things might point to God's presence and what he might be saying to us through them.

It is my hope that this book will speak both *to* and *for* you, prompting you, in turn, more fully to recognise God's presence in the routine business of each day, heaven touching earth such that all of life becomes a prayer.

NICK FAWCETT

1
The alarm clock

It woke me with a start,
   its shrill and insistent beep breaking into my dreams
   and forcing me to stir.
I'd have preferred to ignore it,
   to turn over and go back to sleep,
   but I'd the kids to get to school,
   a bus to catch,
   work to do,
   so I stumbled out of bed in readiness for another day.

Rouse me to your call, Lord –
   your summons to faith, service, repentance
   and commitment,
   however disturbing it may be.
Instead of sleepwalking through life,
   ignoring what I'd rather not face,
   may I hear your voice and wake up to your challenge,
   ready to live each day for you.
Amen.

2
The charity appeal

It was another appeal,
    yet one more begging letter thrust through my door,
    tugging at the heartstrings and seeking my support.
A worthy cause, no doubt,
    as deserving as any other,
    but I'd done my bit, hadn't I? –
    already given more than generously.
What more could people ask?

Is that true, Lord?
Have I done enough?
I've given, certainly,
    but was each donation a meaningful gift
    or a token gesture,
    a response from the heart
    or an attempt to salve my conscience?
I've offered a little but not much,
    what I spare for others over a lifetime
    barely what I spend on myself in a week.
Forgive me,
    and teach me to deal generously,
    as you have dealt generously with me.
Amen.

3
The computer game

I was in control –
    able to shape lives,
    move armies,
    fashion empires,
    influence history –
    and it was compelling stuff,
    addictive,
    like crafting a new world . . .
    playing God.

Only of course I wasn't in control, Lord,
    not in the real world,
    for I'm no more able to dictate my destiny
    than to create life or defy death,
    such a feat beyond my reach.
I can shape things, to a point,
    exerting influence for better or worse,
    but more often than not *I'm* the one being shaped,
    swept along by the latest current of opinion
    or tide of events.
Teach me where true power really lies:
    not in *my* hands,
    but in *yours*.
Amen.

4

The darts match

The crowd waited expectantly as he took aim,
    then sent the dart spiralling towards the board:
    another triple twenty,
    another maximum score.
He'd set his sights high,
    consistently targeting the top –
    and the strategy reaped handsome rewards.

When it comes to discipleship, Lord,
    for all my talk of commitment and sacrificial service
    I set my sights low,
    content to get by rather than excel.
Forgive my limited aspirations and weakness of resolve,
    and help me to aim higher,
    targeting a deeper faith
    and fuller response to your love –
    a life more closely lived with you.
Amen.

NOTES

5

The quality control stamp

It had been rigorously tested,
    checked and checked again,
    declared fit for use
    only after it had met exacting criteria,
    the standards required by quality control.

How would I fare, Lord, were I to be similarly checked,
    my life scrutinised,
    assessed,
    weighed in the balance?
Would I come up to scratch,
    pass muster as a follower of Christ?
I fear not,
    for there's so much wrong in my life,
    so many ways I fall short.
Yet the mystery is that you *do* examine me,
    searching my heart and weighing the spirit,
    and though I fail on innumerable counts,
    still you accept me as I am,
    enough to call me your child.
For that awesome, astonishing truth,
    Lord, I thank you.
Amen.

6
The bicycle

'Have faith,' they said.
'Look up,
  keep pedalling,
  you'll be fine.'
But I didn't believe them,
  for it didn't make sense,
  the bike falling even as they spoke.
I wobbled . . .
  toppled . . .
  and fell.

'Try again,' they said.
'You'll crack it eventually,
  you'll see.'
So I got back on,
  that time . . .
  and the next . . .
  and the next . . .
  until eventually I not only stayed on,
  but did so without thinking,
  cycling suddenly seeming as natural as breathing.

Lord, even when it's hard,
  everything seeming to count against it,
  teach me to keep faith,
  knowing that, however much I falter,
  and however hard I fall,
  you will lift me up and set me back on my way.
Amen.

7
The locked door

It wasn't just closed,
    it was locked and bolted –
    an impenetrable barrier denying access,
    ensuring intruders were kept at bay.

I like to think, Lord, that *I'm* different,
    friendly, receptive and welcoming,
    even to outsiders . . .
    but I'm not.
All too often the shutters go up
    when my view of the world is questioned –
    my mind closed to customs and convictions
    that threaten my own.
Forgive me,
    and teach me,
    instead of automatically locking the door,
    to open it to others,
    recognising that you speak through their words,
    challenge through their insights
    and meet me through their presence.
Amen.

8
The carnival

A carnival atmosphere, they called it . . .
    and it was –
    people dancing and singing in the streets,
    laughing, applauding, chatting and cheering,
    everywhere a sea of exuberant celebration.
For one day, at least, the drabness of life was swept away,
    replaced by a vibrant tapestry of sound and colour.

Lord, I have so much to celebrate,
    yet instead of rejoicing in all you have given,
    the countless blessings you so freely shower upon me,
    I brood over disappointments,
    fret about the future,
    complain about my lot
    and dwell on my troubles
    until I can no longer see beyond them,
    my spirit closed to the generosity of your provision.
Forgive me,
    and teach me each day
    to exult in your awesome gift of life,
    now and for all eternity.
Amen.

9
The cigarettes

She was curious,
    eager to experience, just once, what it felt like,
    so she took a puff . . .
    and spluttered in dismay,
    tears streaming from her eyes.

She was reluctant,
    but her friends were egging her on,
    teasing and goading her,
    so she bought a pack,
    then another . . .
    and another.

She was desperate,
    dying for a fag –
    her only thought
    to satisfy that all-consuming craving within –
    first ten a day,
    then twenty,
    now forty.

Lord, though I can control some things,
    others, if I give them the chance, will finally control *me*.
Teach me to see things for what they are,
    and to act accordingly.
Amen.

10

The broken window

One throw, that's all it took –
   one stone hurled by a thoughtless child
   and suddenly the window was shattered,
   reduced to jagged shards and splintered glass.

So many, Lord, find their lives shattered –
   broken by the loss of a loved one,
   accident or injury,
   the onset of disease
   or the breakdown of relationships –
   and though sometimes they can be restored
   and the pieces put back together,
   sometimes they can't,
   in this life, at least, the damage too great to mend.
Reach out into fragmented hearts,
   bringing healing and hope,
   until that day when your kingdom comes,
   and all is made whole.
Amen.

11
The swallows

They perched on the phone wires,
    rank upon rank of them,
    more arriving each moment
    as though they were preparing for duty,
    responding to a secret summons.
And so they were,
    the voice of instinct,
    impossible to resist,
    calling them to migrate south on another epic journey.

I can't explain your call, Lord,
    for there's so much about it I don't understand,
    so much about you,
    about faith,
    about life itself,
    that leaves me searching for answers;
    troubled,
    confused,
    uncertain.
And yet your summons rings true,
    your invitation to know and love you
    finding an echo in my heart,
    answering some primal need deep within,
    and until I respond I can find no rest.
Help me, fully and faithfully, to commit myself to you,
    and to follow where you might lead.
Amen.

12
The school

They filed through the doors,
    some eagerly,
    some dragging their heels;
    many academically able,
    others with different gifts;
    but, whatever their abilities,
    each would learn something that day –
    each discover more about themselves
    and the world around them.

Teach me more of *you*, Lord,
    and instruct me in your ways.
Open my heart and mind to your guidance,
    and give me a receptive spirit,
    that I may learn to know you better,
    grasping more of your will
    and growing in faith and understanding.
Remind me that,
    however much I have fathomed of your purpose
    or experienced of your love,
    there is more still to discover,
    more than I can ever hope to comprehend.
Amen.

13
The relay race

They were running superbly,
    a gold medal in sight;
    just one more changeover to make
    and victory was theirs,
    triumph assured.
But then, disaster . . .
    the baton fumbled . . .
    dropped . . .
    and the race was lost.

You call me in turn, Lord, to pass the baton on to others,
    handing on to them the message I've received,
    but too often I betray that trust,
    keeping to myself what I should have shared,
    going it alone and forgetting the bigger picture.
Forgive me
    and help me to play my part in your purpose,
    running my leg of the race faithfully,
    so that others may run theirs in turn.
Amen.

14
The icy path

I tried to keep my feet,
    but it was hopeless,
    the ground too slippery to gain a hold.
For each step forward I slid back another,
    my legs giving way beneath me
    as I skidded now this way,
    now that,
    any progress all but impossible.

Lord, I try to walk the way of Christ,
    but I repeatedly slip up,
    temptation and weakness causing me to founder
    and before I know it I find myself back where I started,
    the journey of discipleship more demanding
    than I ever imagined.
Guide my footsteps,
    that I may tread the path of faith more surely.
And should I slide backwards,
    take me by the hand
    and lead me forward again.
Amen.

15
The signpost

It was such a relief to see it:
    to know, after hours of wandering
    and repeated detours,
    that we were back on track –
    with miles to go still, admittedly,
    but at least headed in the right direction,
    on course to reach our goal.

Show me the way I should go, Lord,
    for so often I lose my bearings,
    wilfully taking the wrong road
    or wandering aimlessly through life.
When I mistake the path or stray from it,
    remind me that you are the way that leads to life,
    and may that knowledge guide my footsteps.
Amen.

16
The nightlight

It gave just a glow,
    no more,
    but it was enough to dispel the gloom
    and, with it, the child's fear,
    bringing a sense of security,
    welcome reassurance
    during the dark hours of the night.

Help me, Lord, to glimpse *your* light
    even when life is at its darkest.
Though the night of sorrow, fear, pain or doubt closes in,
    cold and forbidding,
    may a glimmer of your love shine through –
    a glimpse of your presence sufficient to sustain faith,
    nourish hope
    and impart peace.
Amen.

17
The loose change

I pocketed the coins with barely a glance,
    the sum so small it seemed hardly worth counting;
    yet what I judged insignificant
    others would have considered a fortune,
    enough to spell the difference between life and death.
It could have bought food for the hungry,
    medicine for the sick
    or shelter for the homeless;
    but it did none of those,
    lying instead in my pocket
    until spent, not on others, but myself.

Forgive me, Lord,
    for I have received so much yet give so little,
    frittering away money
    on trivia and luxuries I do not need,
    while a multitude suffer and die for want of a pittance.
Remind me of how fortunate I am
    and of all I can do for others at such minimal cost,
    and teach me to respond,
    ready to give not just my small change, but sacrificially,
    just as you gave your all for me.
Amen.

18
The puzzle book

I could work some out easily enough,
   but not others.
They left me scratching my head,
   sitting with furrowed brow,
   bemused and frustrated.
There was an answer somewhere, of course,
   a solution to them all,
   but what it was
   and how to get there
   eluded me completely.

So much in life, Lord, leaves me equally baffled,
   hard to square with faith or reconcile with your love.
Tragedy, pain, injustice and evil cause me to flounder,
   searching in vain for a credible explanation.
Are there answers, Lord?
I believe so,
   and I'll keep on seeking understanding,
   but help me in the meantime to live with questions,
   and to keep faith despite them all.
Amen.

19

The magnifying glass

I was scared for a moment,
    for there among the blades of grass
    were monstrosities –
    hideous and terrifying,
    like nothing I'd seen before.
Yet, of course, they were just ordinary insects,
    ants, beetles and the like,
    magnified beyond recognition.

Forgive me, Lord,
    for I make a similar mistake in life,
    repeatedly magnifying things out of all proportion.
I turn minor weaknesses into major faults,
    disappointments into tragedies,
    and problems into crises,
    trivial disputes blown up into blazing rows
    and innocent remarks taken as personal slights.
Help me to gain a balanced perspective,
    with your help seeing things as they really are.
Amen.

20
The carpenter

I watched spellbound as he worked:
   taking the rough-hewn block of wood
   and turning it on the lathe,
   sculpting and shaping it with gouge and chisel,
   painstakingly transforming the ordinary
   into a work of art.

And I thought, Lord, of the carpenter's son,
   learning his trade in Nazareth;
   of *your* Son,
   nailed to a rough-hewn cross;
   of the young man leaving his father's workshop
   to build instead his Father's kingdom,
   fashioning not just timber but human lives.

Fashion me now, Lord, by the touch of your hand,
   and finish your new creation.
Take who I am,
   and from the deadwood of my life
   craft something beautiful for you.
Amen.

21
The tip

They trawled through the skips
    like eager parasites,
    sifting through the piles of waste
    and setting aside item after item for further use.
What others counted as rubbish, they valued,
    knowing it could be restored,
    recycled,
    reused.

In a world, Lord,
    where so many feel left on the scrap heap,
    discarded by society and of no use to anyone,
    teach me to see the worth not just of objects
    but equally of people.
Open my eyes to look more deeply,
    recognising the gifts, qualities and potential
    of those around me,
    and, wherever I can, help me to nurture them,
    so that they may bloom again.
Remind me that *you* value everyone,
    even if others don't,
    and help me to do the same.
Amen.

22
The judge

It was his job to pass sentence.
Whatever his feelings on the matter,
  his duty was clear:
  not to show mercy
  but to deliver a punishment that fitted the crime.

You, Lord, have cause to punish,
  more grounds for passing sentence than any,
  for I repeatedly flout your will
  and disobey your commandments,
  but your nature is always to pardon.
Instead of holding my faults against me,
  you offer full and free forgiveness,
  the opportunity to start again.
For the wonder of your mercy,
  Lord, I thank you.
Amen.

23
The jury

The moment had come,
    the time for delivering their verdict –
    guilty or not guilty –
    the fate of the defendant largely in their hands;
    but it would be an informed judgement,
    made on the basis of what they'd seen and heard,
    and after careful consideration
    of the evidence presented.

Lord, though I don't like to judge,
    I need sometimes to make up my mind about people –
    not to criticise or condemn them,
    but to assess their motives,
    gauge their character,
    and decide upon the sort of person I'm dealing with.
Teach me to do that wisely,
    not judging in haste,
    still less by appearances,
    nor swayed by hearsay or personal prejudice,
    but impartial in my approach,
    awake to the good and bad in everyone,
    including myself.
In all my relationships, help me to deal fairly.
Amen.

24
The spelling mistake

It was a small error,
  easily missed –
  just two letters juxtaposed,
  but the result was a message very different
  to that intended,
  not just confusing but misleading,
  changing the whole sense of the piece.

I too, Lord, so easily give the wrong message,
  little things in my life,
  seemingly innocuous,
  denying rather than affirming you,
  obscuring your love instead of making it plain.
Alert me to the way I can give mixed messages,
  thoughtless words and deeds, which to me seem trivial,
  in the eyes of others calling into question
  or even undermining
  the faith I proclaim.
Help me to overcome my faults,
  lest they obscure the message of your love
  and lead others astray.
Amen.

25
The thistle

A weed, some called it,
   but it wasn't really:
   it was simply a wild flower
   growing in cultivated ground,
   possessing its own exquisite beauty
   for those with eyes to see.
But to the gardener it was ugly,
   an unwelcome intruder to be grubbed out
   with barely a second thought.

Lord, not everything or everyone is to my liking,
   but save me from dismissing the worth
   of that which doesn't fit my criteria.
Help me to respect the value of others
   and their right to see things differently than I do;
   to understand that beauty is in the eye of the beholder,
   and that just because I fail to see it
   doesn't mean it isn't there.
Amen.

26
The housework

They spoke to me, that day –
    the washing on the line,
    the pile of dishes,
    the neatly ironed clothes
    and the smell of cooking –
    jobs done out of necessity
    but also out of love –
    and as that truth sank home
    I thought of the countless deeds I take for granted,
    small in themselves,
    but contributing so much to my comfort
    and happiness,
    and signifying devotion in a way beyond words.

Forgive me, Lord, for failing to appreciate my loved ones,
    slow not simply to show my gratitude
    but even to notice the innumerable ways
    they enrich my life.
Teach me to recognise everything they do,
    and, in word and deed, to show how much it means.
Amen.

27
The binoculars

I couldn't see *everything*,
   not by a long way,
   but I could see more than before –
   much more –
   details previously hidden from view
   suddenly revealed,
   blurred images brought sharply into focus,
   opening up new horizons,
   possibilities I never even knew existed.

Lord, when it comes to you
   and the things of your kingdom,
   I glimpse only the vaguest outline of reality,
   a mere fraction of the truth,
   yet I confuse this partial picture with the full vista,
   imagining I have seen all I need to see.
Forgive me,
   and open my eyes to the wonder of your presence,
   the fullness of your truth,
   the richness of your love
   and the immensity of your purpose.
Amen.

28
The salary cheque

It didn't seem much –
    scant reward for another month of toil –
    barely enough to cover the mortgage repayments
    let alone feed the family,
    pay the bills
    and have a bit left over for a rainy day.
But what made it worse was knowing that others,
    many others,
    worked no harder yet earned far more,
    able to enjoy luxuries I could only dream of,
    to savour a lifestyle
    that would be always beyond my reach.

It doesn't seem much –
    poor reward indeed for another month of toil –
    but for countless millions it's a fortune,
    enough and more than enough,
    sufficient to meet their needs
    and pay for luxuries undreamt of –
    a square meal, fresh water,
    education and medicine,
    a roof over their heads.

Remind me, Lord, when I feel hard done by,
    of all I have received,
    the many reasons I have to be thankful.
Instead of envying those with more,
    teach me to remember those with so much less
    and gratefully to share from my plenty.
Amen.

29
The speech-recognition program

It was clever stuff,
    the computer recognising my voice
    and typing what I said,
    but, for all its ingenuity, its use was limited:
    it got as much wrong as right,
    more often than not misunderstanding my words
    or misinterpreting my commands,
    the resulting text riddled with errors,
    distorting what I'd intended to say.

Lord, though you speak in a multitude of ways,
    I'm equally poor at getting the message,
    either failing to listen or getting my wires crossed.
I confuse what I want you to say
    with what you've actually said,
    my life, in consequence, a shadow of what it should be,
    marred by silly mistakes and deeper faults.
Forgive me,
    and give me ears to hear
    and a heart to respond.
Amen.

30
The restored building

It had cost a fortune,
    involving innumerable appeals
    and funding applications,
    and there had been plenty to question the wisdom
    of continuing,
    convinced the money could have been
    spent better elsewhere;
    but at last the project was complete
    and the building restored to its former glory.
As the crowds filed through,
    marvelling at its splendour,
    all the time and effort seemed more than worth it,
    a small price for such a spectacular jewel.

Remind me, Lord, of what it cost you
    to restore your broken world,
    the price you so freely paid to make us whole.
Remind me of the immensity of your love,
    the awesome sacrifice
    through which you have made all things new.
I can never repay such goodness,
    whatever I offer in return,
    but I give you my praise
    in grateful thanks
    and joyful worship.
Amen.

31
The shoe shop

There were hundreds there,
    shoes of every shape and size –
    sandals,
    boots,
    trainers,
    stilettos –
    a stunning selection of footwear,
    suitable for male and female, young and old.
And as I browsed along the shelves,
    I found myself thinking of all who would wear them,
    the assortment of people whose feet they'd adorn
    in days to come.

Help me, Lord, to put myself
    into the shoes of those around me –
    not literally,
    but in spirit –
    for only then can I hope to understand them,
    to grasp what makes them tick
    and make sense of their experiences,
    empathising with their hopes and fears,
    joys and sorrows.
Teach me to look beyond my limited horizons
    and narrow interests,
    and to identify more fully with others,
    as you have identified yourself so wonderfully
    with me
    and with all.
Amen.

32
The symphony

It stirred my heart,
    bringing a lump to my throat;
    the emotions it aroused so powerful,
    almost overwhelming,
    that my spirit soared with the melody,
    transported to new heights:
    an ecstasy beyond words.

May the same be true, Lord, of knowing you,
    your presence causing me to catch my breath in wonder,
    to exult and marvel.
Instead of being an arid issue of the mind –
    intellectually assenting to truth –
    may faith be an affair of the heart,
    capturing my imagination
    and transporting me into your presence,
    so that, overwhelmed with joy and filled with awe,
    my spirit may rise to you each day
    in rapturous praise and grateful worship.
Amen.

33
The golf shot

I caught it well,
    better than expected,
    and it soared through the air,
    overshooting the green by a mile
    and landing in the undergrowth beyond.
It had been the wrong club –
    a long iron when a wedge would have done the job –
    and the result was an unplayable lie.

Teach me, Lord,
    to recognise my strengths and weaknesses,
    those things I'm made for and those I'm not,
    and teach me equally to respect the qualities of others,
    open to what *they* can do that *I* can't.
Amen.

34
The dream

I was sorry to wake up,
 for it was a beautiful dream,
 a vision of life as it could and should be –
 touched by peace, joy and contentment,
 obstacles overcome,
 problems at an end –
 and it was a wrench to return to reality,
 to the cold light of day.

Help me to dream dreams, Lord,
 not as a form of escapism
 but in order to glimpse your purpose
 and understand more of your transforming love;
 to catch sight of all you are able to do
 and all I can become;
 to recognise that there is more to life
 than my senses can grasp;
 things too wonderful for me as yet to fathom.
Give me a vision of the future
 and confidence that you will turn dream into reality.
Amen.

35
The compass

It didn't tell me exactly where I was,
    or spell out the path to follow,
    but it helped me get my bearings –
    enough to work out the next step,
    the direction I should take.
And though the way wasn't always easy
    or the path always clear,
    it was sufficient for my needs,
    leading me safely to my final destination.

Thank you, Lord, for the guidance you offer each day,
    not setting out detailed instructions
    for every aspect of life,
    still less dictating the course I should take,
    but prompting through your word
    and pointing the way forward.
Teach me to travel in faith until the journey is done,
    your love a light to my path,
    a compass through the changing scenes of life.
Amen.

36
The spider's web

It looked pathetically frail,
   the silken threads likely to snap
   at the slightest pressure,
   yet, as a hapless fly had found,
   the truth was very different,
   the web like a steel cage,
   escape impossible once snared in its embrace.

Teach me, Lord, never to underestimate *your* strength,
   even when it looks like weakness;
   never to lose sight of the power of love,
   the might of truth,
   or the force of good,
   however much hatred, falsehood or evil
   may conspire against them.
Remind me that nothing in heaven or earth,
   the present or the future,
   will finally be able to frustrate your purpose,
   for you are able to turn sorrow to joy,
   darkness to light,
   and death to life –
   your love stronger than all.
Amen.

37

The water treatment plant

It came in dirty and polluted,
   awash with impurities too many to number,
   yet it went out good enough to drink,
   serving homes across the country,
   fresh water, straight from the tap.

Purify me, Lord,
   for there is so much that sullies my life.
Purge me of all that muddies the waters,
   preventing me from being the person
   you would have me be.
Draw me closer to you,
   so that your cleansing love may flow
   in and through me,
   and make me new.
Amen.

38
The cricket match

It was a difficult time to come in:
    a massive score to chase,
    and wickets having tumbled,
    carelessly tossed away.
One false stroke could have spelt disaster,
    not just for him but also for the team.
But he got his head down,
    dug in,
    and ground out a score,
    only cutting loose when the game was safe,
    his determined concentration
    turning defeat into victory,
    failure into success.

Teach me, Lord,
    that there is a time and place for everything:
    for action . . . and restraint,
    for taking risks . . . and showing caution,
    for enthusiasm . . . and patience,
    for abandonment . . . and self-discipline.
Help me to know which is which,
    and to get the balance right.
Amen.

39
The tree surgeon

It seemed drastic surgery,
   almost brutal,
   virtually every branch lopped off,
   leaving a denuded trunk;
   it was hard to believe such a sorry sight
   could shoot again –
   that fresh growth,
   new life,
   could burst out of the old.
Yet, just a few months later, there it was –
   the tree back in leaf,
   fully restored to its former glory.

Prune the deadwood from my life, Lord,
   and all redundant growth.
Though the process may be painful
   and the measures severe,
   trim back whatever undermines true health
   and wholeness,
   so that I may reach greater maturity in faith
   and become more fully the person you want me to be.
Amen.

40
The zoo

It was a snapshot, that's all,
    a tiny insight into the awesome variety of creation,
    the breathtaking diversity of life on earth –
    animals, birds,
    fish, reptiles,
    insects, and so much more –
    our visit that day offering a reminder
    of the bewildering richness of it all,
    the wonder of our world.

Thank you, Lord, for that special heritage,
    so much to intrigue, entrance, fascinate and amaze.
Teach me to appreciate
    both the privilege and responsibility it represents,
    not only rejoicing at all you have given
    but also respecting its innate worth and dignity
    and playing my part in protecting it for the future,
    so that others may marvel in turn.
Amen.

41
The letter

Hadn't I replied?
I'd meant to,
   lots of times,
   but never got round to it;
   the letter sitting there in silent accusation,
   as though reproaching me for my failure to answer.
I had my reasons, of course –
   distractions, demands, you know the sort of thing –
   but they didn't wash,
   for I'd promised to reply,
   and I hadn't.

Forgive me, Lord, for I mean to answer you –
   to acknowledge your goodness,
   pass on my thanks,
   respond to your call –
   but so often I'm found wanting.
And whatever excuses I make,
   they don't hold water,
   for no concern, however pressing,
   should be more important than these.
Teach me to make time for you
   as you have made time for me.
Amen.

42
The atlas

I knew the countries by name,
   and most of the capital cities,
   and I'd a fair idea of what they were like,
   whether from the TV,
   books I'd read
   or pictures I'd seen.
But that was about it,
   my first-hand knowledge of such places
   being limited to say the least,
   and the bulk of this world,
   in its dazzling diversity,
   something I'll probably never see.

I know *you* by name, Lord,
   and have hopefully grasped
   at least something about you –
   the breadth of your love,
   extent of your mercy,
   power of your word
   and scope of your purpose –
   but save me from imagining I know it all,
   that I've even begun to fathom,
   let alone exhaust,
   the infinite riches of who and what you are.
Whatever I've experienced,
   teach me that there is far more still to be explored –
   enough for *this* life and beyond.
Amen.

43

The road contractors

What a job it was:
    hills to be levelled,
    valleys bridged,
    tons of earth moved
    and debris shifted,
    until finally,
    after months of labour,
    construction could start in earnest.

You've an equally tough job with me, Lord,
    for so much in my life obstructs your purpose
    and prevents you working as you would.
Though I like to think I am growing in faith,
    the truth is you are still preparing the ground,
    making ready the foundations.
Clear away everything that hampers your will,
    so that you can truly build me up
    and finish your new creation.
Amen.

44

The shelter

They'd hardly noticed it before,
    passing it by with barely a glance,
    but when the storm broke and the rain lashed down,
    they noticed it *then*
    and huddled hurriedly inside,
    grateful for its cover.

I'm forgetful of *you*, Lord, much of the time,
    paying you scant heed until trouble strikes,
    only then remembering your love
    and running for shelter in your protective arms –
    a refuge in time of need.
Yet, though I ignore you for so long,
    always you are ready to welcome,
    as faithful as I am fickle.
Thank you, Lord, for being there,
    come what may.
Amen.

45

The stale loaf

It looked all right,
    as good as the day I'd bought it,
    but when I took a bite I realised otherwise –
    the bread dry and hard,
    impossible to eat.

I too grow stale, Lord,
    the freshness that marked my early years of faith
    sometimes seeming a memory,
    a shadow of what it once was and ought to be.
My spirit becomes shrivelled,
    hardened by exposure to the realities of life,
    and I grow set in my ways,
    closed to new ideas and experiences –
    closed to you.
Where discipleship is desiccated
    and commitment withered,
    restore vitality,
    putting a new heart and right spirit within me.
Amen.

46

The shuttlecock

It had no say in the matter,
    no control over events,
    its destiny simply to be smashed back and forth,
    this way and that,
    until finally, unable to endure the pounding,
    it was discarded,
    broken and useless.

Lord, I feel much the same sometimes –
    knocked about by forces beyond my control,
    until I can take the punishment no longer.
Yet you give strength to the weary
    and support to the faint,
    able to see us through
    however fierce the testing.
In the chaos and confusion of life
    I put my trust in you.
Amen.

47

The blossom

I stood spellbound by its beauty:
    a fragrant cloud of blossom transforming
    what had seemed an ordinary tree
    into something breathtaking,
    unforgettable.
But it was more than beautiful;
    it promised fruit to come,
    a rich harvest in the making.

Lord, there is little harvest in my life,
    and that which there has been is nothing special.
But if fruits are missing,
    may there at least be blossom,
    some sign of future growth;
    and though I will always fall short,
    may something of your beauty be seen in me.
Amen.

48

The excavation

Who would have thought it –
   so special a find,
   so rare an artefact,
   hidden so near
   for so long,
   a nondescript patch of earth yielding hidden treasure?

Forgive me, Lord,
   for I judge people by what I see,
   too often failing to delve deeper,
   and, in consequence, I miss hidden gems,
   the pearl within the oyster.
Teach me never to dismiss anyone,
   however ordinary they may seem.
Open my heart instead to the value in all.
Amen.

49
The telephone wires

They hang outside my window,
   hundreds of wires criss-crossing the street
   like a giant cobweb,
   each thread a link to the outside world.
How it works I've no idea,
   but it *does* work,
   allowing interaction that would otherwise
   be impossible,
   bringing together those far apart.

I don't know how *prayer* works either, Lord,
   how you hear or speak,
   how my messages can possibly get through,
   yet, like generations before me,
   I have heard your voice and sensed your presence,
   discovering for myself that you listen and respond.
Though the mechanics are beyond me,
   teach me to treasure your gift of prayer,
   and to use it.
Amen.

50
The flower show

I walked from stand to stand,
    marvelling at the quality of the displays,
    each plant pristine,
    each flower perfect,
    not simply *grown*
    but tended,
    lovingly and painstakingly nurtured . . .
    and the results were plain to all.

Forgive me, Lord,
    for imagining that discipleship can take care of itself;
    that I can sit back and expect faith to grow
    with no effort on my part.
Teach me to work at my relationship with you,
    patiently and with diligence,
    so that you might bring the buds of commitment
    into full bloom,
    and my life to true fruition.
Amen.

51
The weeds

I thought I'd shifted them,
    the weed-killer and trowel having done their job,
    but after a few months they were there again,
    springing up everywhere,
    strangling and suffocating,
    as vigorous as ever,
    and I realised that gaining control
    was not a one-off battle
    but a continuing war.

Teach me, Lord, that I too must be vigilant
    if the tender shoots of faith are not to be overwhelmed.
Faults and weaknesses,
    though conquered for a moment,
    are rarely eliminated –
    each awaiting their moment,
    ready to burst into life when my back is turned
    and take over again.
Save me, then, from complacency,
    and keep me alert to whatever may undermine
    the life you have sown within me,
    so that it may not simply grow
    but, above all, flourish.
Amen.

52
The noisy neighbour

He swayed in time with the music,
   exulting in the pounding rhythm,
   the remorseless throb of the drums,
   lost in the music's power;
   but next door the exhausted baby screamed in protest,
   the mother nursed her headache,
   blinking back her tears,
   and the father hammered despairingly
   on the partition wall –
   so thin a divide between heaven and hell.

In many things, Lord,
   more than I realise,
   my pleasure comes at the expense of others,
   what brings me joy causing them pain.
Teach me, in all I do,
   however innocent it may seem,
   to consider its impact on those around me,
   and, where necessary, to put their wishes
   before my own.
Amen.

53
The fences

There was no doubting its purpose,
    the razor wire saw to that.
'Keep out!' it said;
'No admittance!' –
    a hostile message
    warning people to keep their distance
    or suffer the consequences.
Yet nearby stood another fence,
    encircling a children's playground,
    its purpose very different:
    to protect those playing there
    from the busy road beyond,
    its embrace one of warmth and welcome,
    inviting people in.

What message do I give, Lord,
    and what does it say of you?
Am I open to others
    or closed,
    as approachable as I like to think
    or aloof,
    even dismissive?
Break down the walls I erect –
    the barriers of prejudice, fear, pride and suspicion –
    that my life may reflect your love and openness to all.
Amen.

54
The car crash

He hit the brakes,
   suddenly aware of the danger,
   but he'd left it too late,
   the car skidding out of control
   and smashing into a wall,
   leaving a tangle of wreckage
   from which he was lucky to escape.

Lord, *I* don't know when to stop sometimes.
Whether it's flogging a joke,
   testing someone's patience,
   taking liberties
   or indulging to excess,
   I can push things too far,
   and though I may not see it, damage is done,
   greater than I might imagine.
Whatever I start, Lord,
   help me to know when it's time to call a halt.
Amen.

55
The magnets

They were attracted at once,
    the magnetism almost palpable,
    but when I turned them round,
    they were poles apart,
    literally,
    the one repelling the other,
    and no amount of effort could keep them together,
    the hidden force too strong.

Lord,
    like everyone else
    I'm instinctively attracted to those of like mind,
    resisting those who differ.
But though I know it's natural,
    I know also it's wrong,
    for I need people of opposite ideas
    and contrasting experiences
    to bring balance to my life,
    countering my lopsided view of the world
    and making up what I lack.
However hard I find it to get on with some people,
    inspire me to see beyond what pushes us apart
    to what draws us together.
Amen.

56
The benefit office

The numbers flashed up on the screen,
   summoning 'clients' to the appropriate booth,
   and obediently they responded,
   theirs forms processed,
   their claims dealt with.
Only they weren't numbers,
   they were people,
   with joys, sorrows, hopes and fears,
   just like me.

Reach out, Lord, to those behind the statistics:
   the mother whose partner has walked out
   on her and the children,
   the worker whose factory has closed down,
   the trader whose business has folded,
   the victim of the industrial accident,
   the manager made redundant,
   the casual labourer whose services
   are no longer required.
However hopeless they may feel,
   however disheartened, disillusioned or despondent,
   assure them of their worth as individuals,
   and help us as a society to do the same.
Amen.

57
The pensioner

She looked old and wizened,
    her hair white,
    skin wrinkled and paper thin,
    and youngsters passed her by as if she wasn't there,
    but though the flesh sagged, the spirit still sparkled,
    a youthful zest for life belying the frail exterior.

Give me, Lord, the maturity of age
    yet freshness of youth,
    the wisdom of experience
    yet innocence of childhood.
However many my years of faith,
    may my love for you
    and my desire to know you better
    be as vibrant as the day they were born,
    the life you have put within me, ever old
    yet ever new.
Amen.

58
The sermon

He knew his stuff, I'll give him that,
    and he could probably have recited the Bible
    word for word
    and back to front,
    yet the message left me cold,
    for it stayed up in the clouds
    and never touched down,
    too much concerned with heaven,
    too little with earth.

Lord, set my heart on things above
    but keep my faith firmly on the ground,
    relevant to daily life,
    shaping the things I think and say and do.
Touch the ordinary with the wonder of your presence,
    so that each moment may speak of you
    and be lived in the light of your love.
Amen.

59
The film critic

She tore it to pieces,
    panning the plot, dialogue, effects and acting,
    nothing and no one escaping her attack,
    the film, in her view, not simply a disaster *movie*
    but a disaster through and through.
Was she right?
Who can say?
But it was, of course, her job to pick holes,
    even if she took it to excess,
    her role as critic on the line.

I, Lord, find fault for less reason,
    all too swift to condemn and slow to praise.
I focus on weaknesses rather than strengths,
    faults instead of virtues,
    failure instead of success;
    the negatives swamping the positives
    until I can see nothing else.
Forgive me,
    and instead of dwelling on the worst in people,
    help me to see the best.
Amen.

60

The terrorist attack

It was carnage,
    sickening and horrific,
    like a scene out of hell,
    injuries too awful to contemplate,
    lives, like the twisted wreckage around them,
    shattered beyond repair.
A morning full of promise
    had become the stuff of nightmares,
    yet it was all too real.

Where were you, Lord, when it happened?
What were you thinking of?
How could you let it be?
I look for answers,
    yet search in vain,
    the quest raising more questions than it solves,
    but if one thing is clear, it's that here,
    in this mindless maiming and murder,
    we need you more than ever.
Come to our broken, bleeding world, Lord,
    and bind up its wounds.
Assure us, despite how things seem,
    that hope is mightier than fear,
    right stronger than wrong,
    and love greater than all.
Amen.

61
The sports star

He had it all –
    fast car,
    swank house,
    luxury lifestyle –
but it wasn't simply down to luck.
He was gifted, yes,
    far more than many,
    but he'd honed his skills through patient practice,
    years of hard work belying the apparent ease
    with which he played.

My gifts are less eye-catching, Lord,
    never destined to turn heads or win plaudits,
    but they're gifts nonetheless,
    held in trust for you.
Help me to make the most of them,
    and to use them not just for my benefit
    but for others too,
    consecrating all I am and all I do to your service.
Amen.

62
The Punch and Judy show

They argued and squabbled,
    pummelling each other like spoilt children,
    but, of course, they were only puppets,
    having no life of their own,
    no freedom to choose or will to exercise –
    each controlled by an unseen hand.

Lord, you do not *control* us,
    but have given instead the privilege,
    yet also responsibility,
    of answering for our own actions;
    of being able, at least in part,
    to shape our own destiny.
Help us to do so wisely and thoughtfully,
    mindful of you and others.
Give us humility to respond to your guidance
    but also courage to stand on our own two feet,
    aware of what we *can* do
    and seeking your help in what we *can't*.
Amen.

63

The air-sea rescue

We watched transfixed as the helicopter circled
  and the winch man made his descent,
  dropping inch by inch
  towards the stricken vessel below,
  and then hauling the crew to safety,
  each plucked from the jaws of disaster.

Rescue *me*, Lord,
  for I'm up to my neck in trouble
  and cannot hold on much longer.
Come to my aid
  and lift my head above the waves.
In you alone lies my hope.
Reach out
  and deliver me from the storm.
Amen.

64
The stepping stones

The river was deep and the current strong,
 so, though the stones seemed steady enough,
 I proceeded with care,
 afraid that if I stumbled and fell,
 I'd be swept away
 and dashed against the rocks.

Lord, when I'm uncertain of the way ahead,
 the journey of life presenting unexpected difficulties
 and dangers,
 give me courage to walk in faith,
 trusting you to lead me.
However unsteady my progress
 and daunting the challenge before me,
 teach me to take one step at a time
 and to leave the rest to you.
Amen.

65

The harbour

It offered welcome respite from the worst of the storm,
   boats hurrying for shelter
   from the howling gale and surging waves,
   but when conditions improved
   they were soon on their way,
   out again into open water
   and about their business once more.

Lord, though you promise shelter when the wind blows,
   a haven in times of turmoil,
   save me from divorcing faith from life,
   as though commitment involves running away
   from the world
   and the challenges it brings.
May moments of retreat and quiet devotion
   inspire me rather to fresh service
   and new ventures in faith.
Amen.

66
The window cleaner

I was ashamed when he'd finished,
  appalled that so much dirt could have built up
  without me noticing,
  clouding my vision and obscuring the view.
Suddenly the sun seemed brighter,
  colours enriched,
  little details previously hidden now noticed,
  everything fresh,
  made new.

Wipe clear, Lord, the windows of my soul,
  so that, seeing you better,
  I may know you more fully.
Grant me a clearer picture of you
  that sheds new light on every aspect of life,
  every part transformed by your sanctifying touch.
Amen.

67
The cup of tea

I poured it out eagerly,
    dying for a cuppa to quench my thirst . . .
    but then spat it out,
    grimacing in disgust.
It was tepid,
    neither hot nor cold,
    fit only for the kitchen sink,
    to where it was swiftly dispatched.

Lord, my faith blows hot and cold,
    sometimes setting me on fire with enthusiasm,
    at others, ardour cooled almost to zero,
    but more often –
    too often –
    I'm like that cup of tea:
    lukewarm,
    little use to you or anyone.
Kindle afresh a fire of devotion in my heart,
    and fan there a burning desire
    to love and serve you better.
Amen.

68
The suspension bridge

It was a majestic sight:
    a single graceful arch spanning the ravine,
    simple and elegant,
    yet supporting it were massive chains,
    mighty sinews of steel combining to bear the load.

There are times, Lord, when,
    despite the impression I may give to others,
    I feel weighed down by heavy burdens,
    the pressure building
    until I feel unable to take the strain any longer.
Yet even though *I* can't cope,
    teach me that *you* can,
    your strength sufficient for all my needs.
Help me to entrust myself into your gracious arms,
    knowing you will support me,
    whatever life might bring.
Amen.

69
The new suit

It fitted me well,
    the cut just what I was looking for,
    and I went out that day with a spring in my step,
    feeling good,
    smart,
    transformed.
But I wasn't, of course.
I was no different from the person I'd been before.
The clothes had changed, true,
    but I was just the same underneath as I'd always been.

You speak, Lord of another kind of clothing –
    of gentleness, love, patience, humility,
    kindness and self-control.
Help me not just to toy with such garments,
    trying them on for a moment
    only to discard them afterwards,
    but to wear them each day –
    inner clothes that truly make a difference to who I am.
Amen.

70
The tug of war

It looked easy at the beginning
  as the two teams took the strain,
  each gritting their teeth and digging in,
  but once battle began in earnest, it all changed:
  faces purple with effort,
  sweat dripping from fevered brows,
  tired legs buckling and muscles stretched to the limit
  as a few feet were won,
  only to be lost again.

For all my talk, Lord, of closeness,
  the relationship between us
  is more like a tug of war than shared embrace,
  a broken marriage than match made in heaven,
  for, despite my best intentions,
  I constantly pull away from you,
  resisting your will
  and attempting to impose mine in its place.
Teach me that, however hard I strive against you,
  you will never let go,
  and so may I learn to work *with* you
  rather than *against*.
Amen.

71

The insurance policies

They didn't come cheap,
    but they meant I was covered,
    a policy for the house, car, health and mortgage,
    and just about everything else.
Expensive, true,
    but at least I could relax,
    for I was secure, surely –
    protected against whatever vagaries life might bring.

Only of course I wasn't, Lord, was I,
    for there's no telling *what* tomorrow might bring,
    and however much I try
    to safeguard earthly possessions,
    they can be plucked from me so swiftly,
    this mortal span like a passing shadow
    and my hold on this world tenuous at best.
Yes, I must look after my loved ones,
    ensuring their security as far as I can,
    but remind me of what really counts,
    of the true and lasting treasures found in you alone,
    and teach me to prize those above all else,
    knowing that you are able to keep them safe
    not just now but for all eternity.
Amen.

72
The lichen

How it grew there was beyond me,
    for it was bare rock –
    rough,
    windswept,
    barren –
    yet the lichen had colonised its surface:
    nothing fancy or luxuriant,
    but eking out a living,
    somehow surviving against all odds.

It reminded me, Lord,
    that so many in this world simply *survive*,
    struggling each day to get by as best they can.
Not for them the trappings of life we take for granted,
    the accoutrements we see as ours by right.
They are happy to find even the bare essentials,
    let alone more.
Help me to remember how lucky I am,
    how much I have to celebrate,
    and teach me to respond,
    generously and lovingly,
    so that others may rejoice in turn.
Amen.

73
The glue

It had come unstuck,
    the glue insufficient for the job;
    so I tried again,
    determined that this time the bond would last,
    come what may.

I like to think, Lord, we're indissolubly united,
    but when the glue that binds me to you
    is fear rather than love,
    superstition rather than faith,
    or duty rather than joy,
    then the link is always vulnerable,
    liable to fail when put to the test.
Cement my life through love,
    so that the join is strong,
    able to withstand whatever pressures are put upon it
    and still hold fast.
Amen.

74
The maze

I knew where I was going . . .
    or so I thought . . .
    mastering the twists and turns a piece of cake,
    barely a challenge at all.
But suddenly there was no way through,
    and I found myself retracing my steps,
    coming up against one blind alley after another,
    until, hard though I kept on trying,
    there was no getting away from it:
    I was lost.

When it comes to life, Lord,
    despite the maze of options that daily confronts me,
    I feel confident of taking the right path
    and negotiating my way safely through the labyrinth.
Yet plans have a habit of going astray,
    few things working out as I would like,
    and once more I end up lost and confused,
    uncertain where to turn next.
In all the complexities each day brings,
    the moral and ethical dilemmas,
    the confusing choices and life-shaping decisions,
    grant me your guidance and see me safely through.
Amen.

75
The exam paper

It was a tough paper, no doubt about that,
    so I was pleased not just to pass
    but to pass well.
Yet if two-thirds of the answers were right,
    a third also were wrong,
    much understood
    but plenty more beyond me.

For some reason, Lord,
    questions about you are discouraged,
    as though we either shouldn't have any
    or should know all the answers.
Yet if, even in small things, I have gaps in my knowledge,
    how much more so must it be when it comes to you?
Teach me, recognising your greatness
    and the limitations of my understanding,
    to ask honestly and openly about matters of faith,
    conscious that, however much I have grasped,
    there is always far more still to learn.
Amen.

76
The postcard

It didn't show much –
    just a stretch of hills,
    section of cliffs
    and expanse of sea –
    yet it gave an idea of where we were staying,
    enough to give a feel of the place,
    a glimpse of its peace and sense of its beauty.

Lord, you have given a glimpse of your kingdom
    through the life of Christ and the witness of Scripture.
Not a complete portrait,
    still less every detail,
    but enough to give an impression of its splendour,
    a flavour of the joy, refreshment and tranquillity
    it holds in store.
May that snapshot capture my imagination
    and sustain my faith,
    this and every day.
Amen.

77

The rollercoaster

They were up one minute,
    down the next,
    now slowly climbing,
    now plunging back to earth.
And, of course, it could be no other way,
    each high needing a low and low a high,
    the one counterbalancing the other.

In the rollercoaster of life, Lord,
    with all its thrills and spills,
    teach me to take the ups with the downs,
    recognising that sorrow is sometimes the price of joy,
    and pain the corollary of pleasure.
However deep the troughs or sudden the fall,
    help me to keep faith,
    confident you hold fresh heights in store,
    until I ascend into the fullness of your kingdom
    for evermore.
Amen.

78
The caged bird

It was a sad sight:
    a bird that should have soared and wheeled above
    tied instead to earth,
    not only caged but its wings clipped,
    never again to be unfurled in earnest
    and ride upon the breeze.

There are times, Lord, when *my* wings *need* clipping,
    in order to take me down a bit –
    but save me from becoming so tied to this world
    that I am unable to rise above the petty and mundane.
Liberate my spirit,
    that I may climb to you on eagle's wings,
    catching a vision of what life can be,
    what I can do
    and what you are doing –
    a glimpse of the special in the ordinary,
    the sacred in the secular,
    the divine in the daily round of life.
Amen.

79
The protest march

They lined the streets,
    hundreds of thousands of them,
    banners waving
    like some mighty army going into battle
    as they marched on the city,
    but they brandished words, not weapons,
    their fight being for justice,
    freedom,
    hope
    and truth.

Forgive me, Lord,
    for though I see evil, I keep quiet,
    afraid to speak out
    or too lazy to take a stand.
For all my talk of lofty ideals
    I rarely have the courage of my convictions,
    leaving it instead to others
    to expose wrongdoing and tackle injustice.
Teach me not simply to espouse principles in private
    but to uphold and defend them,
    my allegiance plain to all.
Amen.

80
The kite

It seemed to have a mind of its own,
   leaping now this way, now that,
   up, down, backwards and forwards
   in a frenzy of excitement,
   as if determined to explore every inch of the sky.
But, of course, it was not the kite in control
   but the wind,
   each gust provoking fresh antics,
   new variations in the aerial display.

I *do* have a mind of my own, Lord,
   but I nonetheless find myself tossed around,
   carried along by the wind of change,
   my convictions and principles
   blown about on the breeze
   like so much thistledown.
Anchor my life in your love,
   so that I may think, speak and act wisely,
   the course of my life directed
   by the breath of your Spirit,
   and by that alone.
Amen.

81
The switch

I left it switched on,
    even though I was going away,
    and when I returned a few days later
    it was to find the batteries flat,
    drained of all power,
    no good for anything
    until they had been fully recharged.

I forget, Lord, that *I* need to switch off sometimes
    if I'm not to end up exhausted.
Teach me to appreciate the importance of being still,
    of taking a breather from the demands of life,
    however pressing they may be.
Show me the difference between doing enough
    and doing too much,
    and help me to get the balance right.
Amen.

82
The online update

I'd downloaded the program,
    assuming that once installed
    it would function for years,
    faithfully performing the job it was meant to do;
    but I was wrong,
    for it needed constant updates,
    a regular online search for the latest modifications
    if its usefulness was not to be compromised.

Lord, remind me of the need to connect with you,
    if my faith is to stay fresh and meaningful,
    able to meet the challenge of changing times.
Remind me
    that it is not simply about a one-off commitment
    but about an ongoing relationship,
    the health of which depends on making time
    to hear your voice
    and discern your will.
Install, then, your word on my tongue,
    your love in my heart,
    and your joy in my soul,
    this and every day.
Amen.

83
The starter

It was a mouth-watering selection –
    an array of succulent dishes
    designed to tempt the palate –
    and I struggled to choose between them,
    for each seemed equally appetising,
    too good to miss.
But they were only starters,
    a prelude to the main course,
    a taste, if you like, of things to come.

So much in life seems special, Lord,
    hard to resist,
    and I try to pack as much in as possible,
    afraid of missing out.
Yet however beguiling present joys may be,
    save me from confusing pleasure now
    with treasure to come,
    the attractions of this world
    with the riches of your kingdom.
Remind me that each is but a foretaste
    of the delights you hold in store,
    too many to number,
    too wonderful to contemplate.
Amen.

84
The tent

It wasn't a palace,
    far from it,
    but it was a place to bed down for the night.
And when we were ready to move on,
    it could be rolled up,
    packed away
    and carried with us;
    not an encumbrance
    but an aid to our journey,
    integral to our travels.

Remind me, Lord, that discipleship is a journey –
    not a destination –
    about moving forward:
    exploring fresh horizons,
    discovering new possibilities
    and experiencing yet more of your love.
Save me from getting stuck in a spiritual rut,
    settling for what is comfortable and familiar.
Teach me instead to let go of whatever holds me back
    and to venture out in faith,
    open to whatever you hold in store.
Amen.

85
The joke book

They weren't side-splittingly funny,
    not by a long chalk,
    but they were enough to raise the spirits –
    bringing a smile in place of a frown,
    helping to defuse a tense situation,
    cementing a budding friendship,
    offering a welcome reminder of the funny side of life –
    and in so doing they more than proved their worth.

Though much in life, Lord, is touched by pathos,
    teach me to keep a sense of humour,
    able to laugh, even through tears,
    and smile, even in sorrow.
And though much is serious,
    demanding a measured response and sober judgement,
    help me to retain a sense of fun,
    aware that laughter is your gift,
    as valuable and special as any.
Amen.

86
The wedding ring

It was nothing fancy,
    just an ordinary ring,
    worth little in monetary terms,
    but in terms of the reality it represented, priceless,
    speaking of a love that had stood the test of time –
    of an ongoing relationship,
    enduring commitment
    and bond that would not be broken.

Thank you, Lord, for the relationship I enjoy with you –
    your faithfulness across the years,
    your enduring love,
    your companionship through the journey of life –
    and forgive me that all too often it has been one-sided,
    you having to do all the running.
Renew my commitment and deepen my devotion,
    so that I may respond in kind,
    offering something back to you
    who has done so much for me.
Amen.

87
The tapestry

They were just a jumble of threads –
    no pattern to them,
    no order,
    no anything –
    but, having sketched out her design,
    she painstakingly wove them together,
    creating a thing of beauty,
    a unique and unforgettable work of art.

Thank you, Lord, for *your* creation:
    the beauty of this world and wonder of the universe.
Thank you for so much that speaks of your purpose,
    causing me to catch my breath in awe and wonder.
For the work of your hands
    and all it reveals of your love,
    receive my praise.
Amen.

88
The contract

I'd thought I was covered,
   the contract protecting me in law,
   but as I waded through the fine print
   I realised otherwise,
   the meaning of complex clauses,
   barely understood at the time,
   now becoming clear,
   invalidating the policy.

Thank you, Lord,
   for the contract you have made in Christ,
   the new covenant sealed by his death and resurrection,
   offering new life and love to all.
Thank you that all it asks for is a response in faith –
   no signing on the dotted line
   or assent to complex formulae,
   but a simple act of commitment.
Above all, thank you for honouring your pledge,
   keeping to your side of the bargain
   even though I repeatedly renege on mine.
Amen.

89
The sleepless night

I'd lain there for hours,
  pummelling my pillow and tossing uncomfortably,
  yet I still couldn't settle,
  a thousand ideas turning over in my mind,
  disturbing my peace and denying the sleep I craved.

By day, Lord, as well as by night,
  my spirit is all too often restless,
  unable to find true fulfilment or inner tranquillity.
Help me to let go of my fears,
  and to place every part of life into your hands,
  so that I may know the rest you promise
  and find true contentment –
  a quietness of body, mind and soul
  that, day or night, cannot be shaken.
Amen.

90

The afternoon snooze

I tried to stay awake,
    fighting to control the creeping lethargy,
    but it was no good,
    the heavy meal and glass of wine,
    coupled with the summer heat,
    causing my head to nod and eyelids to droop,
    sleep closing in.

You, Lord, never tire or slumber.
Your love is constant each day,
    your faithfulness ever sure.
Whatever I face,
    you are there watching over me –
    guiding,
    protecting,
    loving,
    forgiving –
    your goodness never exhausted,
    your compassion never failing.
For that assurance, receive my praise.
Amen.

91
The landslip

They looked impregnable,
  mighty cliffs rearing magnificently from the water,
  towering over all they surveyed.
But the battle between sea and rock was one-sided,
  each year another few feet eaten away,
  the waves nibbling relentlessly,
  inexorably changing the coastal scene.

I like to think my faith is impregnable, Lord,
  able to stand up to whatever life may throw against it.
But I know it's not,
  for it too is remorselessly attacked,
  imperceptibly eroded over the years.
Though the assault may be subtle,
  often passing unnoticed,
  the temptation to compromise is always there –
  insidiously gnawing away at my commitment,
  until it's a shadow of what it used to be.
Strengthen my faith,
  that it may stand the passage of time,
  as real tomorrow as it is today.
Amen.

92
The snowflake

Are they really *all* different,
   each flake distinctive,
   unlike any other?
It seems impossible,
   yet that's what I'm told,
   every one of them unique,
   possessing an inimitable pattern that sets it apart.

Remind me, Lord, that people also are different,
   no two precisely the same;
   that though we all have some things in common,
   none of us can simply be lumped together,
   labelled as being of a certain type or particular kind.
Teach me to recognise the individuality of all,
   and to respect each person I meet for who they are.
Amen.

93
The knotted hankie

It was there to remind me, that much was obvious,
    but to remind me of what was less clear.
I'd tried various tricks to jog the memory,
    but each to no avail,
    time and again forgetting vital details,
    special dates
    or important engagements,
    my mind a blank when I needed to remember most.

Forgive me, Lord, for I forget you just as easily,
    your many gifts and countless promises
    slipping from my mind.
Slow to recall your faithfulness across the years,
    I fail to make time for you as I should,
    overlooking your awesome goodness
    and taking your love for granted.
Remind me of all you are,
    all you have done
    and all you are doing,
    and keep such knowledge fresh in my mind,
    each moment of every day.
Amen.

94
The test tube

It reminded me of childhood experiments –
  cocktails of chemicals simmering over a Bunsen burner
  and litmus paper testing strange solutions –
  but it spoke also of complex research,
  of scientists unravelling the mysteries of life,
  creating new drugs,
  fertilising eggs
  and identifying genes –
  unlocking secrets undreamt of in years gone by.

Such powers, Lord, scare but excite me,
  for they have potential for both good and evil,
  able to enrich life or undermine it,
  to transform yet destroy.
Give wisdom to all scientists and researchers,
  and to those who set laws regulating their activities,
  so that the skills you have given
  may be used responsibly
  and to the good of all.
Amen.

95
The children's slide

They ran eagerly into the playground,
    bounding up the steps to the top of the slide
    and screaming with delight as they hurtled down it.
But then one lost control and careered off the end,
    landing heavily on the tarmac,
    where he lay, bruised and shaken.
There were tears, of course,
    but not for long . . .
Almost immediately he was climbing again,
    enthusiasm undiminished,
    such tumbles a price worth paying for the fun.

Sometimes, Lord,
    life brings *me* down to earth with a bump –
    dreams shattered,
    plans frustrated,
    happiness destroyed.
Help me at such times,
    instead of feeling sorry for myself
    and cursing my luck,
    to pick myself up
    and start again,
    knowing that there is no gain without pain,
    no joy without sorrow,
    no laughter without tears.
However often I may fall,
    renew my trust,
    in life
    and in you.
Amen.

96
The radio

It was no good –
    despite all my efforts,
    all my tweaking,
    the signal was poor,
    hopelessly off the frequency,
    at best distorted,
    more often inaudible.

Lord, I find it just as hard to tune in to you.
Though you repeatedly speak –
    calling, teaching, confronting and encouraging –
    I get but a fraction of the message,
    the occasional snippet
    in what is otherwise a sea of noise.
Open my heart to you,
    that I may be more on your wavelength –
    receptive to your word,
    and responsive to your voice.
Amen.

97
The party

They were laughing,
    dancing,
    waving,
    singing –
    and why not,
    for they had something to celebrate,
    cause to rejoice.
Other matters could wait their turn:
    it was time to party,
    and party they did.

Lord, I have cause to celebrate,
    for you have blessed me so richly,
    showering me each day with good things,
    yet I so rarely appreciate it, let alone show it.
I brood, instead of rejoice,
    complain, instead of give thanks,
    my heart heavy rather than dancing within me for joy.
Forgive me,
    and teach me to count my blessings
    and exult in your love.
Amen.

98
The speed bumps

They were a nuisance,
    and I muttered angrily as the car bounced over them,
    shuddering as the suspension took another pounding.
But they did the trick,
    forcing me to watch my speed,
    and slowing me on occasions to a snail's pace –
    the street unquestionably safer as a result.

Teach me, Lord, to take things more gently,
    matching my pace with yours
    instead of hurrying from one thing to the next.
Teach me that it is better sometimes to make haste slowly
    than to rush headlong into a new venture
    and then regret it afterwards.
Teach me the secret of patience –
    the ability to trust in your timing,
    recognising that the journey can be as special
    as the destination.
Amen.

99
The company logo

It spoke immediately,
    one look all it took to call the company to mind
    and everything it stood for –
    suggesting quality and value,
    a product well made,
    worth having.

Though I wear no badge, Lord,
    and bear no label,
    may something in my life speak likewise of you,
    testifying to the love you show,
    the forgiveness you offer
    and the peace you impart.
Help me to point unmistakably
    to your life-changing grace.
Amen.

100
The trampoline

They leapt higher and higher,
  each bounce bringing fresh impetus,
  each downward plunge
  sending them springing upwards,
  soaring towards the sky.

Lord, help me to keep on bouncing back,
  however hard or far I fall.
May I leap up from life's trials and disappointments
  with increased vigour,
  renewed in body, mind and spirit.
May I reach closer to you,
  scaling fresh heights in faith,
  until our hands meet
  and heaven touches earth.
Amen.